THE MISTAKES
MADELINE MADE
BY ELIZABETH MERIWETHER

★

★

DRAMATISTS
PLAY SERVICE
INC.

THE MISTAKES MADELINE MADE was originally produced by Naked Angels (Jenny Gersten, Artistic Director; Seth Shepsle, Producing Director) in New York City, opening on April 23, 2006. It was directed by Evan Cabnet; the set design was by Lauren Helpern; the costume design was by Jessica Wegener; the lighting design was by Tyler Micoleau; the sound design was by Drew Levy; the prop design was by Faye Armon; and the production stage manager was Hannah Cohen. The cast was as follows:

BETH	Colleen Werthmann
EDNA	Laura Heisler
BUDDY	Thomas Sadoski
WILSON	Ian Brennan
DRAKE/JAKE/BLAKE	Brian Henderson

CHARACTERS

EDNA, 23

BETH, late 30s to early 40s

WILSON, late 20s

BUDDY, late 20s to early 30s

DRAKE/JAKE/BLAKE, 20s

PLACE

A basement office in an apartment building in uptown Manhattan.

TIME

2006. Scenes in the bathtub have occurred two years ago, in the bathroom of Edna's campus-housing apartment. In those scenes, Edna is 21 and a senior in college.

NOTES

The play moves without an intermission or scene breaks. All scenes that take place in locations outside of the office are incorporated into the set for the office — for example, Jake can be "frying eggs" inside one of the office drawers. There should be a sense that we are inside Edna's head as much as we are inside an office — or at least that the two are inseparable. The bathtub either sits prominently in the middle of the stage unseen by anyone but Edna, or ideally, it comes in and out, incorporated into the office set. In one production, it was hidden inside different file drawers Edna could pull out at the start of a scene and shut close at the end. As the play continues, Edna should get dirtier and dirtier. (A good trick: hidden hair grease.)

THE MISTAKES MADELINE MADE

Lights come up on an office — two computers, rolling chairs, neatly organized shelves where various toiletries are stockpiled and then stacked with appropriate labels. The organization of the office is extreme but for the right person, probably kind of appealing. Edna, 23, sits spinning in a rolling chair. Beth, older than Edna, sits next to her, typing. Click. Click. Click.

BETH. Edna? Hate to bother you. *(Edna stops spinning and looks at Beth.)* Good news! I have finally received email confirmation that George likes the pair of sneakers we bought — listen to this — I believe he told Judith: "Yay. Mommy. Yay. I love my sneakies." And let me tell you, this kid knows fashion! Give yourself a pat on the back. Come on. Give yourself a pat. *(Edna gives herself a pat on the back.)* Yeah. That's got to feel good.

EDNA. *(To us.)* Take a look at her. Beth. Sometimes I like to think of her in her apartment dressing up like a big bear. Because no one can be like Beth and not secretly want to be taken from behind by a big brown bear.

BETH. Edna?

EDNA. *(To us.)* Grrrr ...

BETH. Now we just need to buy another pair of the exact same shoes, just in case something happens to his existing pair. We call this the "duplicate pair." For everything we buy for the family, we also buy a duplicate, in case anything is lost or damaged in any way. We keep the duplicates down here so we can run up and replace them, if that should ever be necessary. So your job today is buying George a duplicate pair of sneakers. Sound good?

EDNA. *(To us.)* It's not that these are the first rich people I've ever known. No. I went to college with rich people, and we all shared toothpaste. This is different. I am one of fifteen assistants to a family.

This family may be the Platonic Essence of Rich. Their rich is a higher order of being — Money must feel like air, as expected as a breath. It should be called *Mah*-nay. Or Min-*nay*. Dad runs his home the way he runs his hedge fund — using a model to protect his family against the possibility of loss or waste or even just the unexpected. Oh. Oh. I hate them all. But there's no one — There's no one I hate more than Beth. And this hate is rising in me. And it's only been a week. *(To Beth.)* Do you like bears, Beth?

BETH. I collect little china bears.

EDNA. What about big brown bears?

BETH. Oh. No. I don't collect those. Can you find out if New Balance delivers?

EDNA. Balance has two As, right?

BETH. Uh-huh.

EDNA. New Bal-ah-nce. New. Balance. New. Balance. Neeeew —

BETH. How is this working out for you? I know I'm just sort of dropping you in the middle of this, and you're probably not used to the level of perfection that the Household System demands. So I want to emphasize that we're not just buying sneakers —

EDNA. And duplicate sneakers.

BETH. Right. We're not just buying duplicate sneakers, we're George's first line of defense against the whole world! We get in there, we get our hands dirty, we get things done, we buy sneakers, we buy toothpaste, we make sure nothing bad can ever happen to this family. Every day. And I don't know about you, but I think that's what life is all about it.

EDNA. What is life all about?

BETH. These tiny miracles of love. *(A moment.)*

EDNA. When I was six, I had a great pair of sneakers, and then I outgrew them. I was devastated. I ended up roaming the streets barefoot chewing on Q-tips.

BETH. Are you making. A joke? *(Beth stares.)* Don't make jokes.

EDNA. I'm just. I'm trying to get used to this.

BETH. Of course! This is big stuff! But you just got to get in the game and save those jokes for the locker room, okay? 'Nuff said.

EDNA. Where's the locker room?

BETH. Waiter, get this girl a cuppa joe! There's no locker room! I was just making that up! I'm going to have to start calling you "Sleepy"!

EDNA. *(Laughing.)* Don't do that!

BETH. So. New Balance. Silver N. Go!

EDNA. I'll Google it.

BETH. Great! Get on that computer and Google, Google! *(After a moment.)* How's it Googling? *(Buddy, a filthy man in a crumpled suit, sits in a bathtub.)*

BUDDY. I've been, um, I've been having trouble with secretaries.

BETH. What's going on? Are they sold out?

EDNA. Just —

BUDDY. I'm having trouble not killing them.

BETH. Oh God. Car bomb. Look at that woman's face.

BUDDY. I started playing this game.

BETH. Don't there seem to be a lot of car bombs? Maybe they should put all the cars in a parking garage instead of leaving them on the street? Or. I don't know. I'm no expert. God, what a mess.

EDNA. What is?

BETH. You know ... all this fighting? *(The phone rings. Beth picks up the phone.)* Hello, Judith? It's Beth. We're all systems go on the New Balance project. We got one of our best men on it! *(Beth smiles at Edna, give her a thumbs-up. Edna smiles back.)* Check. Check. Unacceptable. Of course, right now. *(Beth hangs up the phone.)* Edna, hey. I'm going to say something. Judith says that yesterday afternoon she asked you to make some copies for her — confirm or deny?

EDNA. Confirm.

BETH. And while you were making these copies, you neglected to copy both sides of the paper — confirm or deny?

EDNA. Deny.

BETH. Edna, you neglected the backside, confirm or deny? *(Wilson enters and stands by the copier, with his back half-turned to Edna and Beth.)*

EDNA. Deny! I copied both sides!

BETH. She says you didn't —

EDNA. I'll go up there right now and check — I'm going —

BETH. *She says you didn't.* Now. Confirm or deny.

EDNA. Ah. Confirm.

BETH. Great, well. I'm not going to blame you.

EDNA. Please. Blame me.

BETH. Of course not.

EDNA. Blame me. Do it. Do it.

BETH. It must have been the copier.

WILSON. Mck-vroo-choo ... Mck-vroo-choo ... Mck-vroo-choo ... *(A slight pause.)*

7

BETH. Nuff said. *(Wilson runs off.)* I'd like you to put together a short email to Judith apologizing. When communicating with Judith, we try to only use words that are absolutely necessary — Judith shouldn't be wasting her time reading a bunch of words! Email me a draft, I'll approve it, and then you can send it. *(Edna types on the keyboard.)*

EDNA. *(To us.)* The system runs like this — I compare it to the world-order Milton created in *Paradise Lost* — God speaks to Adam. Adam speaks to Eve. Thus, for Eve, Adam *is* God. I don't speak to the family and the family doesn't speak to me. When I want God, I go to Beth.

BETH. This is good, but let's cut the sentence, "Oh Judith, after the confusion with the copies, how will you ever trust me again?"

EDNA. Right.

BETH. *(Looking over her shoulder.)* Okay, and here's something — how about starting with "Dear Judith," not "Hey, what's up"?

EDNA. Dear Judith. Dear Judith, I will pay more attention in the future. Dear Judith — *(To us.)* Every day it gets harder to hide my complete incompetence and my love of cock. I haven't always been a slut. I sort of became one after my brother died. I can't stop fucking writers.

BETH. Good! Now, I'm going to give you permission to send this email directly to Judith. So go ahead and click that send button … How do you feel?

EDNA. Lighter. Like the loss of a limb.

BETH. The loss of a limb — you're so wild!

EDNA. How do you feel?

BETH. Oh, I don't know —

EDNA. Say it, anything — how do you feel?

BETH. Like a big chocolate bar that's about to be eaten!

EDNA. With or without nuts!

BETH. *(Enthusiastic.)* With nuts!

EDNA. Yes!

BETH. Hazelnuts!

EDNA. Yes!

BETH. Ha, ha! This is crazy!

EDNA. I know!

BETH. You know, the last girl we had was a real pillbox.

EDNA. A what?

BETH. A real Charlie Reliable. Work, work, work. But I like your spirit. Sure there are times when I need to see a little less spirit and a little more work, but that's why they call me the Lion Tamer.

EDNA. They call you the Lion Tamer?

BETH. Well, I call myself that.

EDNA. You call yourself that?

BETH. I can train anyone. We're going to work from the inside out, Edna. The family wants you to look good and feel good, so you'll work good. I like to think of myself as a role model for the entire staff here — believe it or not, I just never make mistakes! I'm the Lion Tamer — roar! So. Let's get going. What time is it?

EDNA. 2:35.

BETH. What's 2:35?

EDNA. It's um. It's. You told me yesterday —

BETH. Snack time. We need the snack bag dropped off every day in the car so it'll be there when the driver picks George up from school.

EDNA. What's he got in his snack bag?

BETH. I prepared a handout for you in your "George" folder, feel free to follow along ... *(Edna does nothing.)* Okay, we got peeled Asian pears cut in wedges — one-half inch to a quarter inch, a napkin folded once, twice, thrrrrrrice, a small bottle of Poland Spring water, and George's handiwipe. *(Edna picks up a handiwipe.)* No!

EDNA. What?

BETH. You don't touch this. *(Beth takes it out of Edna's hands. Edna stares at her.)* So. Everything goes into a brown paper bag and now I'm going to mark George's name in a black Sharpie on said bag. All caps. George.

EDNA. What if one day he doesn't want a snack?

BETH. Right, right. I'm going to say something: I don't think you're ready for snack time yet. But we're gonna get there and I'm going to make sure we do. 'Nuff said. *(Beth exits with the snack-bag. Edna picks up one of the handiwipes from the box. She holds it and looks out.)*

EDNA. *(Out.)* I'm not supposed to touch this. But. I'm touching it. *(Edna looks around.)* I'm putting it in my pocket ... *(Edna pockets the wipe. Buddy talks from the tub.)*

BUDDY. I just need a couple days. It's normal. I got the front page on my last one —

EDNA. I think Mom —

BUDDY. Under the fold, I mean — I gotta go through my notebooks — I've got about twenty notebooks — just words. It's pretty crazy. And I started doing push-ups. I look great, right? I'm so fucking awesome! Say it — say it —

EDNA. You're so fucking awesome.

BUDDY. Yes. Yes, I am.

EDNA. When did you get back?

BUDDY. Three days ago. Can I have a pillow?

EDNA. Are you going to stay in the bathtub?

BUDDY. Yeah. Yeah. A couple days. Three days. Okay? Four days.

EDNA. Okay.

BUDDY. Great. Thanks. Thanks Edna.

EDNA. I gotta go to class. *(They hug, then just hold each other.)*

BUDDY. When I first got there, they put me in this shitty pool because I was young and they tried to play it off — so I gave it a couple weeks and I just left, got out — got to the city — got a translator — smart as fucking hell. People would just come up to me, they wanted me to write down what they said, they're pointing at everything and telling me to "Write it down!" — I've got like twenty little notebooks, I just wrote till I ran out of pens. This is what I wanted to do.

EDNA. I know.

BUDDY. My whole life. I'm gonna go back.

EDNA. The paper's sending you back?

BUDDY. No. I'm just gonna go. Come with me.

EDNA. You want me to go?

BUDDY. I'm gonna save you —

EDNA. Well, what would we do?

BUDDY. I don't know. We don't have to think, we just go —

EDNA. We could drink dirty water, write novels.

BUDDY. I want you to see it —

EDNA. I've always wanted to write a novel with a big family tree at the beginning —

BUDDY. Your mind just shuts off —

EDNA. We could hide out in a bombed hotel and write epic novels —

BUDDY. And people would hate us —

EDNA. And we'd wear khaki —

BUDDY. Eighteen-year-old guys just shooting goats. Everyone wanted to shoot goats.

EDNA. I want to shoot goats.

BUDDY. Once I tried to get into my car and there was a dead child on my windshield. The guy I was with was like: Hey, it's raining kids. And I was so wasted that there was two seconds when I was like, wait, is it? *(A slight pause.)*

EDNA. Are you going to take a shower?

BUDDY. Enh … *(Buddy lies back in the tub. Drake, a fascinating writer, enters carrying a little notebook.)*

DRAKE. A little of this and that — I've got my fingers in the hot pies, I've always got a couple of doo-dads I'm working on, you know, still wet with the afterbirth of creation — I'll be reading some of them tonight, I've got a couple essays heavily influenced by Kundera — reading Kundera, you know?, it's like slap on the face, like hard, like so hard right on the bone in my face, my face-bone — this unbearable pleasure — I wanted to write him a letter across time, lick the stamp, and say thank you, Milan, thank you for hating me, slash, loving me so hard …

EDNA. Say "Knock, knock."

DRAKE. Knock. Knock.

EDNA. Kuuuundera? *(Edna laughs, Drake doesn't really.)* Drake. Drake?

DRAKE. Yeah. Drake. That's my name. I'm Drake.

EDNA. I'm Edna.

DRAKE. Edna. Are you like angry and self-loathing?

EDNA. Uh-huh.

DRAKE. So what's on your night table? What do you read alone at night to keep the wolves at bay?

EDNA. Oh. Here. *(Edna looks in her bag and holds up a book.)* Joyce Brothers. *What Every Woman Ought to Know About Love and Marriage.*

DRAKE. *(Wagging his finger?)* I smell irony …

EDNA. Can I read you something? You'll love it. It's about the dangers of losing your husband after you give birth. Listen — *(Reading.)* "Take Madeline as an example. Madeline was always so tired after the baby was born that when she and Craig made love, it was a brief, lackluster affair."

DRAKE. Shit, I lost my pot, I think I left it in …

EDNA. Hold on … "Craig found the baby more of a nuisance than a delight. Three years later, he asked Madeline for a divorce. With the mistakes Madeline made by ignoring her husband, she ruined the life she once knew." So what do you think?

DRAKE. That's an essentially misogynistic stance. Dare I say: Duh?

EDNA. Exactly. Which is why I agree with it. Women should be punished — but maybe it's not all women — just certain women — just the kind that use body lotion. We should drag them out to

11

the center of the city and whip them until they bleed. We should stone them alive.

DRAKE. Is this a trick?

EDNA. I find Dr. Brothers' vibrant sense of blame refreshing — I choose to blame Madeline. Madeline is oblivious. Madeline is protected. Madeline is complacent and weak. I will spend my life trying to destroy Madeline. If I can. Legally.

DRAKE. But, listen, listen, what does it mean to be a man? Women are so much deeper. Men have an inherent stupidity, because the erect penis is the root of all comedy. A man with an erection looks himself in the mirror and thinks: Look, it's sticking out, that's funny. The erection is an object that defies logic, like a Cheetoh.

EDNA. So what do you write about, Drake?

DRAKE. What do I write about? I write about kitchens, I write about crossroads, I write about vaginas. I write about the way it feels when the shower runs cold — I wrote a journal entry yesterday. I just sat down to write it. It's called "Explosion — The New York *Times* Changed Its Font."

EDNA. Wow.

DRAKE. *(Rips out one of the pages in his notebook, crumples it up and pockets it.)* God! Just the whole writer thing, arrogance, it's so deeply personal and yet somehow public. I have trouble with that shift. Does it mean I'm afraid of life or … you know.

EDNA. I really like you.

DRAKE. You do? You're looking at me like you hate me —

EDNA. No, no, I'm just clinically depressed. This is my default face. I like you, I do — you write a lot, huh? You just … sit around … and write …

DRAKE. Yeah? You like that?

EDNA. You bet.

DRAKE. What do you do?

EDNA. Um. I completely alienated my parents, we don't speak, and I had to get a job.

DRAKE. Cool, cool.

EDNA. I work for this woman; I hate her.

DRAKE. Right? But what can you do?

EDNA. I want to torture her.

DRAKE. Huh.

EDNA. I want to cover her in dirt.

DRAKE. How long have you been working there?

EDNA. A week. Let's get out of here.

12

DRAKE. I have a girlfriend. She doesn't speak English; she's been sleeping with women. Is that too complicated?

EDNA. You remind me of my dead brother. I'm trying to fuck him back to life. *(A slight pause.)*

DRAKE. Should we leave now? *(We're back in the office. Drake is gone. Wilson stands by the copy machine.)*

BETH. Wilson?

WILSON. Mck-vroo-choo — mck — vroo — choo —

BETH. Wilson?

WILSON. Mck-vroo-choo —

BETH. Wilson, please don't make the sounds.

WILSON. I'm not making the sounds.

BETH. Yup! You are!

WILSON. No. *(A little softer.)* Mck-vroo — sshhhoo —

BETH. Wilson.

WILSON. I'm not making the sounds.

BETH. I know. I know, Wilson. But can you just try?

WILSON. Shhh … *(Wilson turns back around to face the copier.)*

EDNA. *(Whisper.)* Someone said he's writing a dissertation.

BETH. Well.

EDNA. What's it on?

BETH. I never asked.

EDNA. You've never asked? *(Wilson turns back around and stares at Edna.)*

WILSON. Mck-vroo-chooo, chubba chubba.

BETH. WILSON —

WILSON. Yes, I was making the sounds. I was making the copy machine sounds. Yes. *(Wilson suddenly holds up a piece of paper with a large square of purple ink.)* Look — a sunset.

BETH. Wilson!

EDNA. Or a bruise.

WILSON. No. A sunset. I'm Wilson.

EDNA. Edna.

WILSON. Ed. Na. Na, na, na, naaaaaaaa … You know what I love?

EDNA. What do you love?

WILSON. I love making graphs. Or new folders on my computer. I can name the new folder after me. I can call it "Wilson's Folder" or "Wilson's *New* Folder." Or "Wild Wilson's Winter thru Spring Graphs." Point. Click. Double click! I love fax machines. In. Cccch-ccch-ccch-bing! Chho. Out. I love copy machines. Mck-vroo-cchubba, chubba-drroong. And I get to touch these machines every

13

day … Bing! (Wilson stands, staring at Edna.)

BETH. Thanks Wilson … Wilson?

WILSON. I went to the store.

EDNA. Oh. You're still talking to me?

WILSON. I went to get cranberry juice at the store, but they don't keep the cranberry juice in the big refrigerator with the other drinks. It's just stacked up in an aisle. Who is the person who decides which drinks get to be refrigerated and which just get stacked in the aisles?

EDNA. I don't know.

WILSON. I wanted it cold.

EDNA. I love cranberry juice.

WILSON. (Smiling.) Bing! (Wilson runs off. A moment.)

BETH. Wilson has been with the family for a long time. He's the only one on staff that I haven't trained and, to be honest, I think it shows. Some people say he used to work in the hedge fund and there was an accident. Some people say he had a bad childhood. I think he grew up in Florida. You know, in the right light, there's something about him.

EDNA. You think?

BETH. If it's the right light. He's in charge of supervising *The Household Manual*, which explains the Household System. Let me just tell you — I'm a manual junkie. (Beth produces a large book, starts looking through it.) Look — it's itemized — D, D for — well here we got Diapers, we got Disease-comma-Infectious, we got Dishwasher Soap. "Must be organic. Perfume-free." — I love the economy of language, listen to this one: "Purchase bulk over internet." I love that: Purchase bulk. (As she reads this, Wilson runs in with pencils stuck in between his fingers like claws [think Wolverine from X-Men]. He swipes at Beth behind her back a couple of times and runs out.) More manual?

EDNA. I think I'm okay for right now.

BETH. You know — it actually relaxes me? I'm having one of those days. You know. One of those days where you just feel like you're blowing the wrong direction out of the fan?

EDNA. What happened?

BETH. Oh. Nothing. I just woke this morning and I. No. No. If it ain't broke. Ha, ha. But that's when I like to flip through the Manual. Put things back in their proper place. Hey, what about you? You seem a little.

EDNA. What? I'm great. I'm great. It was just a late night. Laaate niiight.

BETH. You went out with a boy last night.

EDNA. Yeah.

BETH. You can talk to me about your boys.

EDNA. My boys?

BETH. You stayed up all night.

EDNA. Yeah.

BETH. Because you were. *(Thrusts back and forth and makes the sound of a creaky bed.)* All night. Same shirt!

EDNA. Uh-huh.

BETH. How was it?

EDNA. Pretty. Standard. Standard issue.

BETH. Were you safe at least?

EDNA. It's never really safe, is it?

BETH. I don't know about that. Sometimes in the heat of the moment, things have their own sort of logic, but I think a good rule to just ask yourself is: Am I doing something that could potentially bring critters into my work environment? *(Edna stares.)* Tuck that away for the future. So, was he … nice?

EDNA. He was a writer.

BETH. Oh, a writer, yes … You know, Edna, I've been with my share. Of men. Not necessarily writers. Sometimes writers. Sometimes collecting unemployment. Sometimes men of the law. A parking attendant. Desmond. A public notary —

EDNA. That's. Great.

BETH. I had some fun times. Fun. Fun. Fun-fun. But I also had. I had some rough times.

EDNA. Uh-huh —

BETH. But, Edna, ask yourself: Why are you doing it? *(A slight pause.)*

EDNA. How was your book-binding class?

BETH. It's a workshop. *(A slight pause.)* Whatever you did last night, it didn't make you happy. Just think about that next time. 'Nuff said. Now we have a job to do. We have to find a purple rug but — this might be tricky — it has to be royal purple, hypoallergenic, and shaped like an octagon. What do you think about that? Let's Google. *(Edna clicks on the keyboard. Stares.)*

EDNA. Cup O' Noodles.

BETH. What? *(We see Buddy in the bathtub eating Cup O' Noodles.)*

BUDDY. Hhmm …

BETH. Edna, what are you doing?

15

BUDDY. There are so many noodles in just one cup. It's extreme. It's like going into the rainforest, but with noodles.

BETH. Edna? Oh look at that. They're just killing each other. What a mess. *(Beth sighs then:)* It's gotta be an octagon. *(Beth leaves.)*

BUDDY. YOU CAN COME IN, SARAH! *(To Edna.)* Tell her she can come in! I'LL CLOSE MY EYES SARAH!

EDNA. Shut up, shut up, shut up —

BUDDY. Sarah came in here like ten times today —

EDNA. It's the bathroom! Buddy, you have to … um. Sarah's my roommate and she's just trying to use the bathroom? We're, like, in the middle of midterms?

BUDDY. Why does she look at me like that?

EDNA. *(Whispered.)* She has a lazy eye. *(A slight pause.)*

BUDDY. OH SARAH, LET'S PUT THAT LAZY EYE TO WORK!

EDNA. Oh my God, oh my God, oh my God —

BUDDY. I LOVE YOU JUST THE WAY YOU ARE, SARAH!

EDNA. *(Overlapping.)* I CAN HANDLE THIS, SARAH, I'M A PEER HEALTH EDUCATOR! She's gone. Buddy —

BUDDY. You're a peer health educator?

EDNA. Yeah, why? *(A moment.)*

BUDDY. So you *are* a virgin.

EDNA. No, I'm a trained active listener. I work the eating disorder hotline on Fridays.

BUDDY. That sounds depressing.

EDNA. You're not allowed to say depressing, unless you know what depression is. I'm allowed to say it because I'm a peer health educator.

BUDDY. I slept in your bathtub last night, I think I can use "depression" in a sentence. *(A slight pause.)*

EDNA. My professor … told me … we've been talking about stuff in class … about this idea of, um, these-Christian-fascist-ideologues-removing-the-divide-between-Church-and-State? And how that's affecting foreign policy and that's going to be really bad? Um. Are your nose hairs like falling out?

BUDDY. It relaxes me.

EDNA. What — like smelling yourself?

BUDDY. Kinda. Yeah. But enough about me. What's going on with you?

EDNA. Stressed out. You know. Gearing up for midterms. Raa! And I'm a peer health educator. I'm like the best.

BUDDY. Yeah? How do you know you're the best?

EDNA. Well, the peer health educators are going into local high schools to do skits about date rape, and I got the lead. You want to help with my lines?

BUDDY. No —

EDNA. Come on. The highlighted parts are my lines. Start at the top of the page.

BUDDY. *(Reading.)* "Hey baby."

EDNA. "Hey Kevin."

BUDDY. It's "Hi Kevin."

EDNA. It doesn't matter. "Hi Kevin."

BUDDY. "There's a big party tonight at the Kappa house. There's going to be a lot of alcohol and, uh, drugs. You're going to the party, aren't you?"

EDNA. "I don't know if I should, Kevin."

BUDDY. "It's a kegger. And there will be lots of drugs."

EDNA. "Should I go?"

BUDDY. "Come on, baby, if you don't go, you're not going to be cool. And I won't go out with you anymore."

EDNA. Wait, wait — "If you're going to put those limitations — "

BUDDY. Boundaries.

EDNA. "If you're going to put those boundaries on our relationship, Kevin, then I don't think you care about, um, my belief system"?

BUDDY. Perfect.

EDNA. There's another page, there's an alternative ending where she goes to the party and gets date-raped —

BUDDY. You know that part?

EDNA. It's all like, "Stop, no, stop." We do the skit and then they decide what choice she should make — They discuss it. It's like choose-your-own-adventure.

BUDDY. I think you're going to change the life of a local high school student.

EDNA. Yeah?

BUDDY. No, this has the opposite effect, it actually makes you want to go the party and get date-raped. I mean, *come on* — write your own. Use some imagery. Is it a big keg? What kind of beer is it? Why is his name Kevin?

EDNA. It's just — it's Kevin.

BUDDY. What if it were more evil, like Otto?

EDNA. No one is named Otto, it's not plausible.

BUDDY. Otto Von Bismark, Otto Dix, Otto — Otto Heinrich Warburg —

EDNA. You're so annoying!

BUDDY. Or you could call him Fat Hands?

EDNA. My hands are proportional. Monsterface.

BUDDY. Fat hands.

EDNA. You have stupid facial hair.

BUDDY. Your knuckles are like tiny children.

EDNA. How'd you get through customs without showering? Were you wearing a hat?

BUDDY. You think you have to shower before you can reenter the country?

EDNA. I don't know — you can't bring back cheese from France.

BUDDY. Maybe they didn't know how dirty I was.

EDNA. Or maybe you were wearing a hat. Come on, get out of the tub — you're not really going to sit there, right? *(A slight pause.)*

BUDDY. You know date-rape doesn't sound so bad. Comparatively speaking.

EDNA. What do you mean? Compared to what? *(Jake, a poet, suddenly enters in boxers holding a spatula.)*

JAKE. Heeeeey, morning.

BUDDY. I'm going back —

JAKE. What?

BUDDY. Come with me —

EDNA. What?

JAKE. It's Jake — Jake —

EDNA. Right, sorry.

JAKE. I'm making iz-eggs all up in he-ah.

EDNA. What?

JAKE. I'm making eggs.

EDNA. Oh. That's not. Necessary.

JAKE. Eggs. Breakfast. Hunger. *Bi-otch. (Jake picks up a notebook and jots down these new ideas.)*

EDNA. Jake?

JAKE. Right. Jake. Remember? You kept telling me you wanted to ride with me? You were like: "What's a bitch gotta do — "

EDNA and JAKE. *(Remembering.)* "To ride wit chu."

JAKE. Yeah! You remember.

EDNA. Yeah.

JAKE. You're so cute, with that button nose all ova ya face — Button nose — wha' wha'! Gimme that button nose, giirrrrl — *(He playfully goes after her nose —)*

EDNA. Aaaaah!

JAKE. Gimme that nose, girl — *(He grabs her and squeezes her nose, Edna is laughing.)*

EDNA. Aaaaah — Monsterface —

JAKE. What'd you call me? — Oo — *(He takes out his notebook. As he's writing:)* "She be calling me monster face, like monster is my faaaace — "

EDNA. Don't write that.

JAKE. What's wrong? *(Edna is breathing hard.)* How 'bout I put cheddar cheese all up in your omelet?

EDNA. Last night —

JAKE. Yeah, sorry I didn't come. I'm on like a shitload of anti-depressants. Anti-depriz-nats! Did you?

EDNA. No.

JAKE. Well, you just lay there. You should try to get into it. Slap my ass a little. Shit like that. You should talk more.

EDNA. You should shut up sometimes.

JAKE. Hey I'm going to let these simm-ah, and hop in the shiz-ower —

EDNA. The what?

JAKE. The shower. Come with?

EDNA. Come with you?

JAKE. Aw baby, it'd be so niiiiice. Get the Dove bar all under ya arms —

EDNA. No. *(Edna is staring, breathing hard. A moment.)*

JAKE. It's not like a big deal.

EDNA. You're a terrible poet.

JAKE. Huh. Well, I'm not a poet, I'm a man who rhymes.

EDNA. Your poems make me ashamed to speak English. So. I'm just going to find my underwear.

JAKE. It's over there. Where you threw it. So.

EDNA. Yeah. *(Beth enters with a box, and we're back at the office.)*

BETH. EDNA! The handiwipes are here!

EDNA. *(To herself.)* "What's a bitch got to do, to ride wit chu?"

BETH. What's a bitch got to what? Did you make the label?

EDNA. Here. *(Beth sniffs.)* Did you just sniff at me?

BETH. Get your head in the game. There's no hyphen in handiwipe.

EDNA. Well, it's not really a word, is it? Handiwipe is not really —

BETH. Judith spells it without a hyphen, so —

EDNA. Do you want me to get a dictionary? I'm getting a —

BETH. *Judith spells it without a hyphen.*

EDNA. I'll make a new label. *(Edna starts to make the label on the label machine.)*

BETH. Edna, hey. I'm going to say something. Are you happy here? Do you want to have fun? Come here. Take a look at these. I bet you don't know a thing about these handiwipes.

EDNA. Confirm.

BETH. Did you know George's skin is incredibly delicate? If he touches the wrong kind of fruit, he can die.

EDNA. Wow.

BETH. It took me three weeks on the phone every day before I found these in a small factory in Appalachia. I wrote Judith a report comparing this brand with twelve other brands. She never read it, she just told me to buy them, sight unseen. That's when I knew Judith finally trusted me. And I was happy for the first time in a long time. Think about that. Do your job, and you'll be a happier person. I know, okay? Nuff said. *(Edna goes behind Beth's back to take a wipe, Beth spots it and swats it out of her hand.)*

EDNA. Ouch —

BETH. Don't take a handiwipe from a six-year-old boy. *(A slight pause. Beth takes out a bottle of lotion from her drawer. She rubs it in.)* I'm tough. I'm a stubborn little lady. I'm the Lion Tamer, Edna. And this job is going to turn your life around if it's the last thing I do. Nuff said. *(Beth exits. Edna grabs handiwipes, laughing.)*

EDNA. *(Overlapping.)* I'm doing it, I'm doing it —

WILSON. Tweet, tweet! *(Wilson runs in. Edna is caught with piles of handiwipes in her fists.)*

EDNA. Oh geez. Wilson.

WILSON. What are you doing?

EDNA. I don't know — I just — I think I'm taking her handiwipes and I'm holding them hostage. I think that's what I'm doing. So you can tell her or you can not — tell her — what's it going to be?

WILSON. Aaaaaiii.

EDNA. What's it going to be? Are you in?

WILSON. I'm in! Ha, ha. *(Wilson laughs and grabs handfuls of wipes.)*

EDNA. I hate her.

WILSON. Me too. Meeee toooo. I hate her.

EDNA. I hate her so much.

WILSON. I hate her so so much. ChhhhhhvvvvvvvvvvRING!

EDNA. What's that?

WILSON. That's how much I hate her.

EDNA. What did she do to you?

WILSON. She doesn't like my sounds.

EDNA. I like your sounds.

WILSON. You like my sounds? *(Edna nods. A moment.)*

EDNA. You want to know what the scariest thing is?

WILSON. Yes, I do want to know what the scariest thing is.

EDNA. There's a part of me that likes to file.

WILSON. Sometimes it's nice. Filing. Sometimes. Uh. Hiiii. Edna. Na. Na.

EDNA. Hi Wilson.

WILSON. Handiwipes are funny. Why? Go!

EDNA. The word. It's a funny word.

WILSON. Yes, handiwipe. Handiwipe.

EDNA. You go!

WILSON. Handiwipes are funny because, because you're carrying around a little wipe so you can wipe yourself — that's just funny, period. That's really funny.

EDNA. Who actually uses handiwipes?

WILSON. I know someone. There was a woman on a plane I sat next to. Do you have time for a story? Yeah? Okay? It's kind of interesting. So I was flying from New York to Detroit, and I like to fly because of plane sounds — Like: Ffffeeeiiirr —

EDNA. Yeah —

WILSON. Yeah, okay. Whoops. Shut up Wilson. And the woman started to talk to me even though I was sitting there making sounds to myself. She was a sales rep for a stationary company — Imprintables — what are imprintables? Imprintables, imprrrrrintables. Aaaah — Bing, bing, okay. She's coming back from New York where she was at a stationery conference in the Javitz Center. Boring, boring. And she didn't like to be in New York alone. And I told her that I am always alone and she told me to try internet dating.

EDNA. Did you?

WILSON. Uuuuh, no. No. I. I don't have successful blind dates.

EDNA. Okay, yeah.

WILSON. Vrrroooo. My story races ahead. So her kids asked for T-shirts — from the MTV store and from the Hard Rock Café. And she's Armenian. She liked the movie *My Big Fat Greek Wedding* and she talked about how her family was like that movie, except big, fat, and Armenian, but I didn't see that movie so then she decided to explain the plot to me in a lot of detail. This was the sound of her voice, if you took out the words: EEEEE, neeka, neeka, EEEEEE, gropop.

EDNA. Wilson, Beth is coming back soon —

WILSON. No, no, wait — her nephew was in the army fighting. And she had been a mother to him because his mother died of breast cancer when he was in high school and — snap! He doesn't graduate, joins the army, and goes over and fights and she sends him care packages but he doesn't respond. She tells him it's a waste of time and energy. He finally responds. He says hi, how are you, and then he asks her to send handiwipes. That's all he asks for. If I were in the army, I would ask for Oreos.

EDNA. Of course, me too.

WILSON. But he asks for handiwipes. And I told her. Maybe he just feels like his hands are always dirty ... *(A slight pause.)* Do you know what I like most of all? The way a plane sounds when it lands. Very ... complex ... Did you enjoy my story?

EDNA. I did. A lot.

WILSON. Dong, dong, dong. *(A slight pause.)*

EDNA. What's that?

WILSON. That? That was my special bell sound ... I've been waiting to tell that story for a long time. It kind of just sits there in my head. Do you have that? This story that just lives in your head?

EDNA. Yeah, I have that.

WILSON. Yeah?

EDNA. My brother. Lives in my head. The week he came to visit me. He's dead. He's — he is no longer with us. He is not of this earth. I don't know how to say it. I have syntax problems. He was killed a year ago.

WILSON. Hhhhooo ... oohhh ... Edna —

EDNA. You don't have to make your sounds. I'm fine. It's fine. *(A slight pause.)*

WILSON. Hhhooo —

EDNA. Stop. Seriously. You sound like an owl. *(A slight pause.)*

WILSON. My paper. My paper lives in my head.

EDNA. The dissertation?

WILSON. The. Big. One. I've been working on it for a long time. Long time. Ha, ha. Woo.

EDNA. What's it on?

WILSON. Leibniz. Monads.

EDNA. What?

WILSON. Leibniz's perceptual monads. The definition of the soul. Tiny bubbles of soul. *(Revving up his engine.)* Vrrrrooooo ... *(In a funny mechanical voice.)* The soul is the tiniest place that is capable of memory — the soul is any tiny space where multiple moments of time can exist at once. *(He snorts.)* NEERRRRD.

EDNA. Wow. Tell me more.

WILSON. Okay, it's my favorite thing to talk about. *(Revving up his engine.)* Vrrrroooo … We have no concrete definition of memory, so there could be tiny bubbles of soul everywhere. What if there's memory in a copy machine or an old shirt … Or just a speck on the ground … so if we destroy anything, if we sweep the floor, are we killing tiny pieces of soul? How could we live that way, and also we wouldn't be able to do chores. So there has to be some things that can be thrown away or forgotten … And this is the problem with our power — how do we decide what to destroy? Do we forget about the copy machine? I don't want to forget about the copy machine.

EDNA. Uh-huh.

WILSON. But if we forget about the copy machine or throw out the shirt or, to get more abstract whhoooo, if we pretend like we don't know something is happening, if we forget about it, then it isn't really alive anymore … This is the nature of our power — just by ignoring it, we can kill it … Fffff! Dead … So what do we choose to forget? *(A moment.)* I don't know. I don't have a thesis.

EDNA. Do you have a bibliography?

WILSON. I have a working title.

EDNA. Let's hear it.

WILSON. "Tiny Bubbles of Soul." You like it?

EDNA. Yeah.

WILSON. Ming, tingy-ting! *(Wilson takes out a pocket notebook and writes something down.)*

EDNA. What are you writing?

WILSON. I'm working on something new — What's that smell?

EDNA. What smell?

WILSON. Like rotten something. Like rotten —

BUDDY. You're a baby, you think like a baby —

EDNA. *(Overlapping.)* Hey, get out of here, hide these — *(Wilson stares at her.)*

WILSON. It's you. You smell. *(Wilson runs out with the bag.)*

BUDDY. Look at us! We're a country of babies and secretaries —

EDNA. What does that mean? That's like one of those things you say and everyone thinks it's really smart —

BUDDY. There were probably ten thousand women systematically raped last year in Pakistan, and Pakistan receives a billion dollars from the United States to fight terrorism, and you're doing a skit about date rape.

EDNA. You can't say that a girl getting date-raped in the United States is not as bad as a woman —

BUDDY. No one knows what's happening, this is modern warfare — these are guys just pushing buttons — we're just pushing buttons-how do you get your mind around that —

EDNA. I think we do know what's happening-

BUDDY. No, no, no, no, no —

EDNA. *(Overlapping.)* Listen to me — listen — you're not listening to —

BUDDY. *(Overlapping.)* Look at you, you're pushing buttons —

EDNA. I'm not pushing buttons —

BUDDY. *You're pushing buttons, you fucking baby.*

EDNA. Buddy. *(A slight pause.)*

BUDDY. Yeah. That was not.

EDNA. I figured out what you have. Ablutophobia. The fear of bathing. The inability to bathe due to extreme anxiety.

BUDDY. Jesus Christ —

EDNA. — The majority of cases take place in America. I looked it up yesterday. I read a couple books, you know, about life-threatening experiences? I might try to write an essay or something — like "Ablutophobia and America-on-the-Brink"? There's usually some trigger, have you been under a lot of stress in the past month? *(Buddy stares at her.)* Yes. Okay. Were you ever around a loud explosion? Did you see someone you know die? Were you ever afraid that you would die? When is the last time you showered?

BUDDY. You think my arms look bigger?

EDNA. Like fatter?

BUDDY. No, the muscles are defined or something. Like, you can really see the individual muscles.

EDNA. Oh God, you smell so bad!

BUDDY. Can I be honest with you? I have become jacked. I'm *jacked.*

EDNA. Let me just turn on the water —

BUDDY. No, no. Just.

EDNA. Okay. *(A slight pause.)*

BUDDY. I can't stay here and have all these little conversations — these little topics, here's what I think and my ceiling's been leaking, and what do I want and I love my new cell phone and that's a picture of my dog, and everyone loves my dog, and do you want to see more pictures of my dog and these little conversations I have to have — I want to kill secretaries. It's normal. It's normal, after your first big trip it just takes some time to readjust.

EDNA. You want to kill secretaries?

BUDDY. I got back to the paper and there were secretaries everywhere. I forgot we had so many secretaries. What do they do all day? Do they go home and watch TV? What do they think about? And I played this game where I made guesses on which secretary was most likely to survive an attack and which one would end up running around the office on fire. And then Grace. *(Beth enters.)*

BETH. Do you smell something? *(Beth exits.)*

BUDDY. Grace had pictures of dogs. They were so ... strange.

EDNA. What, like, weird dogs?

BUDDY. No, just ... dogs. Like: Dog faces. Like dog noses? Big close-ups of dog noses sitting in, you know, grass or something. And I just couldn't — why? Every day? Every day you're going to look at a dog face and you're going to rub lotion on your hands and talk to me about your dog? Like the dog threw up today and I didn't know what he ate? My second day back she put up a life-size cutout of Derek Jeter made out of freestanding cardboard. It just stood there next to my desk. We were near the kitchen. My third day back, it was her birthday and someone gave her a nightgown — like a black nightdress — She took it out in the middle of the newsroom. People started hooting. I was also hooting.

EDNA. You were hooting?

BUDDY. Yes, I was one of the loudest hooters. But I know there's a knife in the kitchen I could take out pretty easily. I could take it out pretty easily, stab her in the gut, get my coat, and take the elevator down to the lobby. So I went to the kitchen but then I'm face-to-face with Derek Jeter, and I could see him swinging his bat and hitting Grace on the head. I know the sound she'd make. And he hits her again and she's laughing because she loves Derek Jeter, and he hits her again, and blood's coming out of her mouth, and I opened the kitchen drawer. And then I closed it. And then I started yelling. I think I started yelling. And I came here. Because I was yelling. I think I was ... yelling.

EDNA. Okay. That's okay.

BUDDY. They suggested I take some time off.

EDNA. Okay.

BUDDY. I can't stay here.

EDNA. So I'll come with you. I'm coming with you.

BUDDY. Yeah? *(Edna itches herself. Beth enters.)*

BETH. There's a smell.

EDNA. Uh, uh.

BETH. Hm.

EDNA. Hm.

BETH. Huh. Huuuuuh. Huh. I have to go upstairs, why don't you figure out what smells?

EDNA. Um-hm ... *(Beth exits. Edna looks around. Whispers.)* Wilson! Wilson! *(Wilson enters stealthily with tissues in his nose.)*

WILSON. Sshhh ...

EDNA. She's gone — *(Edna takes handiwipes from the box and gives them to Wilson.)*

WILSON. Hey Edna —

EDNA. *(Overlapping.)* Shhshh —

WILSON. *(Whispered.)* I'm enjoying this handiwipe caper.

EDNA. Me too. Are you sick?

WILSON. Do you think I'm sick?

EDNA. You have tissues in your nose —

WILSON. It's just easier this way.

EDNA. What's easier?

WILSON. Nothing.

EDNA. So where have you been hiding the wipes?

WILSON. Everywhere, like little stars in the sky —

EDNA. You're hiding them individually?

WILSON. After work.

EDNA. You stay after work to individually hide the handiwipes —

WILSON. It's a delicate process. *(Edna holds up a handiwipe. She laughs.)*

EDNA. Look, last one.

WILSON. Ha, ha ... Last one.

EDNA. Are we going to do this?

WILSON. Yes.

EDNA. Yes!

WILSON. Yes, I think we're going to do this. *(Beth enters.)*

BETH. Wilson, what are you —

WILSON. Shug, bugschug — *(Wilson runs out.)*

BETH. God, what is that smell?

EDNA. Maybe it's you?

BETH. Oh, methinks not ... *(Beth squirts some lotion onto her hands. Before she closes the bottle, she waves her hand over the top to get some lotion smell out into the air.)* Here — have some — I love this lotion — I love it — Here, it's made out of avocados — *(Beth pours a little dollop into Edna's hand. Edna stares at it.)* You got to rub it in ... *(Edna shakes it off, with force, into the trash.)* I'm going to say something: Do you regularly shower —

EDNA. No, I don't.

BETH. Okay, what can I do? Should I come over some Saturday afternoon —

EDNA. *(Sharp.)* You're not coming over. *(A slight pause.)*

BETH. I don't want to have to fire you, I like you, Edna. I don't know why but I do. Maybe because I *was you.* Crazy. In pain. Pants around my ankles. You're young and pissed off, and you want to be free, so you dye your hair and you get pregnant. *(A slight pause.)* And you get pregnant but that doesn't even matter. There are no rules, nobody cares ... So you let people hurt you. I know about the darkness. But I kept working and it felt better. It did. Just take care of the smell.

EDNA. It's 2:35. I got the bag ready. *(Edna hands her the snack bag.)*

BETH. Look at that smiley face in the "O." That's great, Edna. What about the handiwipe? *(Edna puts her hand in the box and finds no handiwipes.)*

EDNA. Oh no.

BETH. What?

EDNA. No more handiwipes. *(Beth looks in the box.)*

BETH. We just ordered some. I never run out. I've never ... run ... out.

EDNA. It's 2:35.

BETH. He has a piano lesson — *(Beth gets down on her hands and knees and starts looking.)* I ordered them, I know I ordered them, I ordered them, George has a piano lesson —

EDNA. Oh no. Sticky fingers. *(Beth looks at her.)*

BETH. Oh my God.

EDNA. What?

BETH. Did you do this? Did you take them? Is this a joke?

EDNA. Ha ha.

BETH. You're fired!

EDNA. So fire me. But what will you put in George's snack bag? It's 2:36.

BETH. Where are they?

EDNA. All of them. Hordes of them. Hundreds of handiwipes. Hidden. Somewhere. Somewhere in these very offices.

BETH. My God.

EDNA. I'll give you one per day. I'll give you one for every snack that needs to go in the car. You can withhold my paychecks, but you'll have to ask me politely every day: "Edna, may I have a handiwipe?"

BETH. You're a monster!

EDNA. One per day until a new shipment arrives. And then you can fire me —

BETH. I was nice to you; I wanted to help you —

EDNA. 2:37. 2:37 and five seconds. Six.

BETH. Please?

EDNA. I thought you were the Lion Tamer.

BETH. Give me a *(Whispered.) fucking handiwipe* —

EDNA. Wilson!

BETH. Wilson? Is Wilson in on this? *(Wilson enters.)*

WILSON. Zzzzzooom.

BETH. You would do this to me, Wilson?

WILSON. *Et tu,* Wilson?

EDNA. The lady wants a handiwipe.

WILSON. *(In some weird voice.)* The lady wants a wipe!

BETH. Wilson, where are they?

WILSON. Shhh … *(Wilson exits like a sneaky cat.)*

BETH. I know this office inside and out, I know every place you could hide a handiwipe, I'll find them. *(Beth starts to open the cabinets — there is an overwhelming amount of stockpiled drug store products in all of them.)*

EDNA. You don't stand a chance. *(Wilson enters with a handiwipe.)*

WILSON. *(As Santa?)* Merry Christmas, Beth! Ho, ho — handiwipe!

BETH. Wilson. Stay. Sit down.

EDNA. Don't sit down.

BETH. Sit, Wilson.

WILSON. Hmm …

BETH. Wilson. You know where the handiwipes are? Confirm or deny.

WILSON. Confirm … And deny.

EDNA. Beth, it's 2:38.

WILSON. 2:3-eeeeiiiggght. *(Beth grabs the handiwipe.)*

BETH. Don't tell anyone about this — *(Beth exits.)*

EDNA. Ha, ha motherfucker!

WILSON. Neeeeeiiiirrrr — pssshoo — bang! She's toast.

EDNA. I'm going to fucking destroy her, Wilson, I'm going to fucking destroy her.

WILSON. Whoa. You're really angry.

EDNA. So what?

WILSON. When you get angry, I can see the muscles in your cheeks. Which reminds me. I want to tell you something ...

EDNA. *I'm so fucking awesome!*

WILSON. Forget it ... Baaaaaaa ... *(Wilson runs out. Blake, a writer of short stories, enters and Edna grabs him. They make out.)*

BLAKE. Did you like the reading?

EDNA. Uh-huh —

BLAKE. I get so nervous —

EDNA. Uh-huh.

BLAKE. I'm a writer, I'm not supposed to talk in front of people. You know, my words are supposed to talk for themselves ... or ... why are they words? This is hot — It's like you heard my short stories and you just had to have me — that's so hot — I'm like a rock star, but also a short story writer — *(They're totally making out.)* What is that smell —

EDNA. Trash.

BLAKE. Hot — it's like we're cats in an alley —

EDNA. Like a tomcat —

BLAKE. Or an ... alley cat.

EDNA. Kiss me.

BLAKE. What's that smell?

EDNA. *Shut the fuck up. (A moment.)*

BLAKE. Um.

EDNA. I just. I don't smell anything, Blake. Blake?

BLAKE. Yeah, Blake ... You know what? I think you're lonely.

EDNA. Yeah?

BLAKE. It's okay. You can tell me you're lonely. We're so afraid to say that sometimes. Let's say it together. Come on. On three: one, two, three.

EDNA and BLAKE. I'm lonely.

BLAKE. Yeah. That was good.

EDNA. Are we going to have sex?

BLAKE. Sure. Okay. This is an alley.

EDNA. Yes or no —

BLAKE. I mean, I've just had a long-term kind of thing. I'm in the middle of a break-up. You know? And it's like, what could be worse than breaking someone's heart?

EDNA. Attacking them.

BLAKE. Huh. I think that piece was also about Iraq. You know? It wasn't a coincidence that I broke up with Meeka the same weekend the shrine was destroyed. Can you give me a back rub?

EDNA. I don't really do that.

BLAKE. Oh ... I think maybe I should —

EDNA. Wait —

BLAKE. I'm just not — I'm not the kind of guy who does this kind of —

EDNA. You're a tomcat —

BLAKE. Yeah, no. I'm not. But I'm never going to forget this — I mean —

EDNA. You said you were lonely, I'm lonely too.

BLAKE. I got to go —

EDNA. Hey Blake, I'm lonely!

BLAKE. I gotta — *(Edna pushes him hard up against the wall.)* Ouch —

EDNA. I'm lonely, I'm lonely — *(Blake, trying to get away, pushes Edna so that she falls on the ground.)* Aah!

BLAKE. Are you okay? Oh shit, crap, shit, crap, crap — *(Blake runs out. Edna is still on the ground.)*

EDNA. I'm lonely. *(We hear Buddy screaming. Edna goes to him.)*

BUDDY. Edna. I'm not. Doing so good.

EDNA. Shhh ...

BUDDY. Was I screaming?

EDNA. Sarah wanted to call the cops, I told her to fuck off. I think she's taking the semester off.

BUDDY. How long was I screaming?

EDNA. About a half an hour. You said "fuck" a lot.

BUDDY. I don't know what's happening to me.

EDNA. We're going to get out of here — I'm going to help you get your notes together. I bet you have great stuff. You're going to write a book, we're going to help people. We're going to be like the brother-sister reporter tag team. We can wear matching hats. *(Buddy stares at her.)*

BUDDY. You don't know anything.

EDNA. We don't have to wear matching hats.

BUDDY. I thought you would.

EDNA. We can talk — talk to me.

BUDDY. I'm lonely.

EDNA. But I'm here, talk to me. I'm going to help you, I'm going to learn more. I'm going to read some books, I'm going to figure it out —

BUDDY. Yeah? What are you going to do? Are you going to write a skit about it? *(Beth enters, covering her nose with her shirt, and starts to make up a snack bag.)*

BETH. It's 2:35. You smell terrible. It's just. It's terrible. Now please give me a handiwipe.

EDNA. Bomb falls next to you, what do you do, Beth? What happens? Come on. It's like choose-your-own adventure.

BETH. I'm asking you nicely, Edna.

EDNA. It's actually like someone's pushing hard on your back — I've been doing a lot of reading — the majority of casualties are caused by people bleeding to death.

BETH. You said all I had to do was ask you for a handiwipe, so I am asking you, politely, may I have a handiwipe?

EDNA. Someone is next to you, bleeding, what do you do, Beth? Do you run?

BETH. It's 2:35. WILSON!

EDNA. I want to see you run.

BETH. I need a handiwipe.

EDNA. I want to see you run, Beth. I want see gas pouring down on you —

BETH. You want to see gas pouring down on me? Really? I don't think you do. *(They stare at each other.)* I know about your brother, Edna. *(A moment.)*

EDNA. Wilson told you.

BETH. Google. Sounds like a tragedy. I'm sorry for your loss. Now, it's 2:36. I'd like a handiwipe. Please. *(Wilson enters with a wipe.)*

WILSON. Doo-doo-doo. I am the King of the Handiwipes! *(Beth takes the wipe from Wilson, she exits.)* Edna? She's gone. Edna? Got a hat on, huh?

EDNA. Yeah? What? Why?

WILSON. Hat attack! *(Wilson pulls Edna's hat over her eyes.)* Gotcha. Hee, hee, hat attack ... Did you like, "I am the King of the Handiwipes"? Because I've been thinking a lot about the things I say when I come in with the wipe — I thought "Merry Christmas" was pretty good. What about, "Here's your wipe, bitch?" Eeeee. I kind of want to call her: Beth Breath. Beth Breath.

EDNA. Get the tissues out of your nose.

WILSON. No, I can't. But I was wondering. Ummm-hmmm. I love the handiwipe caper. It makes me feel like I'm walking on stilts all over everyone, crunch, crunch. I feel like a man ... And you're a. Woman and women are fine. But you are. A different kind of woman. *(Wilson coughs a little.)* Whoo! It's a little hard to, uh, breathe.

EDNA. Smell it, Wilson. *(Wilson takes the tissues out of his nose and starts to cough and gag.)*

WILSON. Whoo-ooo-aaaagggh — Edna …

EDNA. Smell it.

WILSON. Aarrggh —

EDNA. Don't pretend I'm someone I'm not.

WILSON. Aarrrggh, whoo — I wanted to know if you wanted to have a coffee with me —

EDNA. I don't shower, Wilson.

WILSON. Well. Turn on the water.

EDNA. I can't, I can't just turn on the water.

WILSON. Is it your electric bill?

EDNA. I don't shower.

WILSON. Oh. Well, I'd like to see you. Um. If not for coffee maybe we could go swimming. Or I. I would just like to spend a day with you if that's okay … Is that something you would find appealing?

EDNA. Why don't you just fuck me right here on the floor?

WILSON. No, I thought we could just go out —

EDNA. You thought I liked your sounds and I was nice and you could take care of me —

WILSON. *(Overlapping.)* No, no, hey. I want to. Jeeesh.

EDNA. Take off your pants, Wilson! *(Edna dives for his pants —)*

WILSON. Don't touch my — eee —

EDNA. Take off your pants and fuck me or I'll kill you — *(Wilson guards his pants. Edna backs off. A moment.)* He was enormous. He was ten-feet tall.

WILSON. Your brother?

EDNA. His body came back in pieces.

WILSON. Hhhhoo.

EDNA. I have this little life, I have this little, little … I have this … life, Wilson … and I don't know what to do with it … I have … life … I have … life … I have this …

WILSON. I think you're … enormous. *(Wilson reaches out to touch her.)*

EDNA. I would rip you apart.

WILSON. Okay.

EDNA. I would hurt you so bad.

WILSON. So maybe we can get coffee some time?

EDNA. What's going to happen, Wilson? Are you going to love me? Are we going to *love* each other?

32

WILSON. I don't know —

EDNA. You can't even finish a paper, you can barely speak English — what do you think we're going to do together —

WILSON. *(Overlapping, starting after "a paper.")* Frrrrrrring, taka, taka, taka, frrrrrrring —

EDNA. I don't want to be around you — I'm forced to be around you, because we work together, but I would never choose to be around you, Wilson —

WILSON. *(Overlapping.)* Gegegegeg — taka, taka — ggrreeeee taka taka —

BUDDY. I'm going back in the morning.

WILSON. Gggggggg —

EDNA. *What is that?*

WILSON. I don't know. It's inside me. *(Wilson runs off.)*

BUDDY. I'm going back. Edna.

EDNA. Let's go —

BUDDY. Edna.

EDNA. I'm coming with you. I'm gonna pack —

BUDDY. Come on. You can't go with me, I can't keep you safe —

EDNA. I don't want to be safe — I want to do what you do —

BUDDY. You can't.

EDNA. Yes I can.

BUDDY. You have this life, you have this little life —

EDNA. But I don't want it —

BUDDY. Yes you do —

EDNA. No! I've got a midterm tomorrow, and I'm not even studying! I'm not doing my homework! I've never not done my homework! I don't even know how to not do my homework — I'm going to fail! I'm going to fail and it doesn't even matter!

BUDDY. Edna. What are you going to do tomorrow? You're going to take a midterm. No, first, you're going take a shower, and everything will fall off of you, everything that stuck to you, everything that splashed in your face and the air is warm and wet and it smells like fruit, and it'll just fall off you — the chemicals, the black water, dead hair, the blood —

EDNA. I want to see it —

BUDDY. No. No. I want you to know what you do — I just want you to know. You do it, every day, you stand in the shower and forgive yourself and you don't even know what you're forgiving yourself for, you are so ... blind ... We did this — all of us — we all did this and you can let yourself be clean, you can do that, you can

33

stand in the shower — You can let yourself, you can let yourself be clean — *(Buddy gets out of the tub and walks off. Edna is crouching on the floor. A moment. Beth enters holding a big brown box.)*

BETH. Edna? Get off the floor. Edna —

EDNA. I'm fine.

BETH. You're. Um. You're on the floor. Gasping.

EDNA. I'm fiiine.

BETH. Well. The new handiwipe shipment arrived. It's right here — Oooo, heavy. *(She puts the box down.)* So the jig is up. You got me. You really did. It was quite an operation. And there may even have been parts of it that I enjoyed. But you clearly have a lot of problems that you need to work out. I don't know how to help you and also I'm pretty angry at you, so. You know, bad things happen but you get up in the morning and take a shower and come to work and there is nothing wrong with that — I tried to understand, Edna … *I tried.*

EDNA. I know …

BETH. You do? Because you're so. Hard on me, Edna. I've never met someone who hates me so much. I mean I'm not really the kind of person people spend time *hating* … I'm annoying, sure … but I've never been *hated* … I don't know what to make of it. Just knowing you're out there, even on the weekends, you're out there, somewhere, hating me. It sort of makes me crazy. It makes me wonder if you were sent here to make my life miserable. But that doesn't make sense. Because you seem more miserable than I do. Edna?

EDNA. I'm not. Doing so. Good.

BETH. No, no, don't do this — let's get off the floor — *(Wilson enters.)*

WILSON. I have something to say. Oh hello Beth Breath.

BETH. Hello, Wilson. Just to get you up to speed: The new shipment arrived. Edna's on the floor, and I just fired her.

WILSON. Hhhhhooo …

BETH. Did you call me Beth Breath?

WILSON. What did you do to her?

BETH. I don't know. I don't know what I did.

WILSON. Edna? *(Wilson begins to open the new box of wipes.)*

BETH. That's the new box. That's the new shipment …

WILSON. I know it is, Beth! *(Beth looks at Wilson.)*

BETH. Well, don't rip it. If you're going to open it. Use scissors. *(Beth hands Wilson scissors. Wilson opens the new box. Wilson takes out a wipe.)*

WILSON. Edna ... Give me your hand. *(Edna doesn't move. Wilson reaches out for Edna's hand, she pulls it away.)* These ones. These are the safest in America. Ha, ha.

EDNA. Wilson, I'm not. Doing. So.

WILSON. *(Overlapping.)* No. No, don't do that —

EDNA. *(Overlapping.)* Wilson. I don't want to forget him.

WILSON. Just ... give me your hand. Please. Give me your hand. *(Edna does. Wilson holds Edna's hand and starts to wipe it with the handiwipe.)*

BETH. This is. This is crazy ... *(Wilson holds up the used handiwipe. It's very dirty.)*

WILSON. Take a look at that, ssshhho!

BETH. Wow. *(Wilson gets more wipes from the box.)*

WILSON. Let me have your arm —

EDNA. I don't —

WILSON. Arm. Arm — *(Wilson starts to wipe Edna's arm.)*

EDNA. Wilson —

WILSON. Shhhh ... *(Wilson is done with the arm, drops that wipe. Goes for another one.)* Move your hair, okay — *(Edna holds her hair up as Wilson starts to wash her face, her neck.)* I like your neck ...

EDNA. Ahah — *(Edna is breathing hard, the action disgusts her and relieves her.)*

WILSON. It's okay — just — there — okay, okay, okay, okay — *(Something is released in Edna, she is relieved, shaken, crying.)*

EDNA. Aaaaahhhh ... *(Wilson throws the last one down. Edna stares at Wilson. A long moment. They sit there. It is not uncomfortable, but it's not comfortable.)*

BETH. Well. *(A slight pause.)* They didn't dry you out, did they? *(Edna shakes her head.)* So good. They're not supposed to dry you out. Good.

EDNA. Beth ...

BETH. We forgive ourselves, Edna. I don't know if we should, but we do. *(A moment.)* I have to go upstairs to talk to Judith. I expect you to be gone when I get back. Both of you. And you can take that box with you.

WILSON. Thank you.

BETH. Well. I have three more coming tomorrow. *(Beth exits. A moment.)*

WILSON. I just put my thesis through the paper shredder —

EDNA. The whole thing?

WILSON. And the disk it was saved on. The shredder broke. But

I've been working on something new ... um ... it's uh ... uuuuu-uhhhh ...

EDNA. Wilson, I better get out of here ...

WILSON. Wait, I want to show you. What I've been working on. *(Wilson opens a thick pocket notebook and reads from it.)* The Edna Notebook. Volume 1. Item 1. Edna. She wears pretty sweaters. She introduced herself to me. I made funny noises. Item 2. Stop making funny noises. Item 3. Is it possible that I have fallen in love with Edna? Item 4. Yes. Item 5. Observe, research, come up with hypothetical solutions to the problem. Weigh the possible consequences of each proposed solution and then choose one. Choose one, Wilson. Choose one. Act. Item 6. Stop making funny noises. *(Wilson flips through the book.)* Item 55. She only wears one bra. I know because when she takes out the trash every day, the sweater moves in such an angle that I can see her bra strap. Every day it is the same color. It doesn't quite fit her because she is always shifting it with her hands. That would mean she has worn the same bra, a bra that doesn't fit her, for fifteen days in a row. Why? Does it smell? Do breasts sweat? Check this. *(Wilson flips through the book.)* Item 78. Her shoulders get tense when she's lying. Watch for this. Note: I will be able to win a lot of money from her in a poker game if this should ever be necessary. Item 79. You don't even know how to play poker, Wilson. Item 80. She talks to me more when I don't shave. Note: Don't shave. Does this mean she wants me to look more disheveled? Refers to someone she met over the weekend as Junkie-Poet-with-the-Big-Cock. Note: See if you can ask her not to talk about him like this anymore. Item 81: Try to figure out why she dated the Junkie Poet. What does she want? Item 82: Clicks her tongue when she's organizing her things. As in: "I put my keys in my bag (click), and there's my wallet (click), and my address book, pen (click-click)." Scary. Item 83: I like when she laughs. Item 84: Try to think of some interesting stories. Note: The story about how I went to buy the cranberry juice went over well. What about the handiwipe story? Item 85. Is it possible to love someone so much who you can't speak to? Item 86. Yes. *(Wilson flips through the book.)* Item 204. When did she stop showering? Will this be a problem in the future? (See breast-sweat question.) Item 205. She smells terrible. Item 206. One hundred wipes. So far. Item 207. Trying to remember if her hair was up or down today. Was distracted by her smell. I can't remember. I have to remember. I have to write it down. *(Wilson flips.)* Item 245. She yelled at me. Is this what it feels like to die? Item

246. Probably not. Item 247. I hate monads. Who am I kidding? Item 248. Chcchchchch. Parenthesis — sound of paper shredder. Close parenthesis. Item 249. Regret about destroying years of work for a girl who just yelled at me. Item 250. You can't save everything, Wilson. Item 251. Chhhhhchuckchuckagrrrrrrrrrccccck. Parenthesis — noise of a paper shredder breaking — close parenthesis — *(Wilson flips to the end of the book.)* Item 256. Going next door to kiss her. I've never been good at kissing. Bing, bong, bung. Item 257. If I can't make funny noises, am I allowed to write them down? Item 258. She's alive. And I am so. I am so. Ha. Ha. I'm so glad. Item 259. Item 259. *(Wilson stares at Edna.)*

EDNA. I tried to take off your pants —

WILSON. I know. I know that.

EDNA. I'm not always. Like that, I just.

WILSON. It's been a while since anyone's tried to take off my pants ... You smell better. A little bit.

EDNA. Item 259 —

WILSON. I don't know how I feel about Item 259. It's. *(Edna kisses him.)* That was. That was.

EDNA. Dong. Dong ...

WILSON and EDNA. Dong ...

End of Play

PROPERTY LIST

Handiwipes, boxes of handiwipes
Snack bags
Notebooks, pens
Book
Copy paper
Manual
Pencils
Cup O'Noodles
Script
Spatula
Label machine
Bottle of lotion
Tissues
Scissors

SOUND EFFECTS

Email ding
Phone ring

NEW PLAYS

★ **RABBIT HOLE by David Lindsay-Abaire.** Winner of the 2007 Pulitzer Prize. Becca and Howie Corbett have everything a couple could want until a life-shattering accident turns their world upside down. "An intensely emotional examination of grief, laced with wit." *–Variety.* "A transcendent and deeply affecting new play." *–Entertainment Weekly.* "Painstakingly beautiful." *–BackStage.* [2M, 3W] ISBN: 978-0-8222-2154-8

★ **DOUBT, A Parable by John Patrick Shanley.** Winner of the 2005 Pulitzer Prize and Tony Award. Sister Aloysius, a Bronx school principal, takes matters into her own hands when she suspects the young Father Flynn of improper relations with one of the male students. "All the elements come invigoratingly together like clockwork." *–Variety.* "Passionate, exquisite, important, engrossing." *–NY Newsday.* [1M, 3W] ISBN: 978-0-8222-2219-4

★ **THE PILLOWMAN by Martin McDonagh.** In an unnamed totalitarian state, an author of horrific children's stories discovers that someone has been making his stories come true. "A blindingly bright black comedy." *–NY Times.* "McDonagh's least forgiving, bravest play." *–Variety.* "Thoroughly startling and genuinely intimidating." *–Chicago Tribune.* [4M, 5 bit parts (2M, 1W, 1 boy, 1 girl)] ISBN: 978-0-8222-2100-5

★ **GREY GARDENS book by Doug Wright, music by Scott Frankel, lyrics by Michael Korie.** The hilarious and heartbreaking story of Big Edie and Little Edie Bouvier Beale, the eccentric aunt and cousin of Jacqueline Kennedy Onassis, once bright names on the social register who became East Hampton's most notorious recluses. "An experience no passionate theatergoer should miss." *–NY Times.* "A unique and unmissable musical." *–Rolling Stone.* [4M, 3W, 2 girls] ISBN: 978-0-8222-2181-4

★ **THE LITTLE DOG LAUGHED by Douglas Carter Beane.** Mitchell Green could make it big as the hot new leading man in Hollywood if Diane, his agent, could just keep him in the closet. "Devastatingly funny." *–NY Times.* "An out-and-out delight." *–NY Daily News.* "Full of wit and wisdom." *–NY Post.* [2M, 2W] ISBN: 978-0-8222-2226-2

★ **SHINING CITY by Conor McPherson.** A guilt-ridden man reaches out to a therapist after seeing the ghost of his recently deceased wife. "Haunting, inspired and glorious." *–NY Times.* "Simply breathtaking and astonishing." *–Time Out.* "A thoughtful, artful, absorbing new drama." *–Star-Ledger.* [3M, 1W] ISBN: 978-0-8222-2187-6

DRAMATISTS PLAY SERVICE, INC.
440 Park Avenue South, New York, NY 10016 212-683-8960 Fax 212-213-1539
postmaster@dramatists.com www.dramatists.com